William de Goat

William de Goat

Squadron Leader Brian Waite RAF

ATHENA PRESS
LONDON

WILLIAM DE GOAT
Copyright © Brian Waite 2008

All Rights Reserved

No part of this book may be reproduced in any form by photocopying or by any electronic or mechanical means, including information storage or retrieval systems, without permission in writing from both the copyright owner and the publisher of this book.

ISBN: 978 1 84748 283 9

First published 2008 by
ATHENA PRESS
Queen's House, 2 Holly Road
Twickenham TW1 4EG
United Kingdom

Printed for Athena Press

Contents

Preface	vii
Foreword	ix
Out of Jail	11
Gravesend	19
Wild in Lincolnshire	25
Left Behind	33
Typhoon Boys	41
Relief in the Air	49
Into Europe	55

Preface

I was privileged to command 609 (West Riding) Squadron from 2001 to 2006 and as a consequence, became a reader of the history of this famous Royal Auxiliary Air Force Squadron. It has an illustrious past, in particular during the Second World War when it was engaged in the retreat from Dunkirk, the Battle of Britain, D-Day and the advance through Europe during 1944–45.

After forming at RAF Yeadon – now Leeds/Bradford Airport – in 1936 and early days on the Hawker Hinds and Harts, it entered the Second World War flying the Spitfire. During 1942 it replaced the much-loved Spitfire with the Hawker Typhoon. Much has been written about the exploits of the aircrew in particular, and the ground crews, however as I read books on the squadron and spoke to veterans, the name William de Goat regularly entered the conversation. The mascot was to be with the squadron from 1941–1945, very nearly without a break. This creature intrigued, even fascinated me and my research followed. The result of this research is *William de Goat*, a history of the four-legged creature that was to become the highest-ranking officer to serve with 609 (West Riding) Squadron.

Foreword

Brian Waite's charming Novelette *William de Goat*, featuring the 609 (West Riding) Squadron mascot makes delightful reading, all the more so since William in his own words tells us about his experiences with the squadron.

I first met William in October 1943, just after he had been promoted to group captain by Squadron Leader Pat Thornton-Brown in celebration of 609 Squadron's 200th victory in the air. It did not take me long to establish that William preferred to chew my cigarettes rather than be stroked or be treated like a pet, which was quite understandable since as the official mascot of the squadron he felt it was below his dignity. So we had a cordial if not overly-close relationship, sharing my cigarettes from time to time. Any petting was left to the squadron dogs in my care — first, 'Blitz' and later, 'Tiffy'.

Group Captain William de Goat DSO, DFC was well aware of his duties as the squadron mascot in boosting the morale of the pilots, even if at times he was moody and only reluctantly attended the squadron photo calls. However, he was an essential part of the establishment and often in dangerous situations and I do not know what we would have done without him.

My best wishes for the success of this charming story.

Sir Kenneth Adam OBE

SIR KEN ADAM left Germany in 1934 as Klaus Hugo Adams, with his German Jewish family. It was therefore with the greatest persistence that he got himself accepted firstly into the RAF and secondly into a combat role – for it would not have been a POW camp for him.

He changed his name to Keith Howard Adam just before joining 609 in 1943, and was known as 'Heine' on the squadron. He changed his name again to Ken after the war.

Since the end of the war he has become well known in the world of theatre and cinema as an artistic director. He created the war room in *Dr Strangelove* and was credited as Artistic Director on seven of the *Bond* films. He was awarded two Oscars for his work on the films *Barry Lyndon* and *The Madness of King George*.

He was knighted in 2003.

Out of Jail

Where was I born? Why was I born a goat? I was meant to be somebody special, not some*thing* special. So why a goat? Still, I was more special than most goats, or was it that I had more opportunity than most goats? Who knows... but what *was* I doing in the Old Jail pub in July 1941? Ah, the Old Jail... What a place – just up from Biggin Hill where that damned Belgian pilot was flying at the time; his name was Ortmans, but more of him later.

So, anyway I was born a goat, address unknown. From photos you can see that I was born of the species, British Goat – more specifically a British Toggenberg. I was cute, without doubt, all fur and with the stubs that were to later become very famous horns. I never knew my mother and father, probably victims of that terrible thing that was happening at the time, that terrible thing that was to influence my life – us goats did not know about war, it was humans who did that kind of thing.

But I was a goat and that dear landlady, Biddie, of the Old Jail was destined to wean me until, in a moment of madness – or was it the passion of war – she handed me over to Vicki of the Ortmans variety. Vicki had a way about him; the weaning was over; life was taking over – or was it madness?

The Old Jail public house was a gathering point for the Belgians and Frenchmen on the squadron. Biddie was from Belgium and apart from the draw of the language, she had a radio which received news from home, and of course she had a fine wine cellar...

In July 1941 I arrived at Biggin Hill, home to something called aircraft, which were attached to something called squadrons, which were attached to men. Some men took them into the air, some did not. It is at this time that I assumed superiority over all other goats. I began to understand, and treat with some disdain, the humans who thought they had adopted me. Little did they know that it was *I* that was adopting *them*.

It was the men of 609 (West Riding) Squadron, Royal Auxiliary Air Force who I had decided, somewhat by default, or passion, to adopt. They already had an illustrious history but little did they how much I was to enhance it.

One morning, Vicki introduced me to the men who took the Spitfires, that is the name I had heard the boys calling their aircraft, into the air; some smiled, some ignored me and some tried to rub their hands on my head and stroke my fur. I tolerated it because they fed me and watered me. I will refer to these as the boys, in fact I will often refer to them as *my* boys — for that is what they were. These boys were mainly officers, they flew the aircraft and sat around when they did not. The men lived in another place and worked near the aircraft thing — they did not have time to sit around. Why I was with them, I didn't really know at this stage but the word 'mascot' was often mentioned.

Now, the goat definition of a mascot is, 'thing believed to bring good luck to its owner', but I did not agree with 'owner'. I owned them, and with some luck that was to become clear to them too.

So, what about my boys? They looked after me when they were not sitting in the Spitfires, which amazingly, from a goat's perspective, could fly. Now, I had seen birds fly before and envied them their freedom, but a man in a machine — flying? They called me William de Goat, the 'de' because Vicki, a Belgian, had adopted me. They also painted something on my small horns; there was one thin circle on each side — I was Flying Officer William de Goat… but I could not fly.

Anyway these boys were a real mixed bunch. There were Englishmen from something called the upper classes; there were Belgians, Frenchmen, Americans, Canadians, Australians and New Zealanders. They were all here to fly the machine that was to defend my country. Some ignored me, some looked after me, that's the way it was. I was young and still learning the ways of a goat, never mind the ways of these humans. I had to be fed and watered frequently; Ortmans saw to that. Books on goats tell you that we need to be fed a balanced diet, including types of grass, hay, minerals and vitamins, but I don't think Vicki or any of the others read any relevant books. After a month on milk, which was not easy to acquire, Ortmans transferred me to beer — easier to get hold of. It was better than milk even out of a bottle; I was too young for a glass. Food was anything I could scrounge — grass from the field, flowers from wherever they grew and scraps of anything the boys brought me. I was not destined to be hungry and my special four-compartment stomach enabled me to cope with most things they gave me.

The four-compartment stomach was vital to William and enabled him to sustain his life, despite the extraordinary diet he was to endure for the next four years. Briefly, food is passed into the first two compartments for partial digestion before being regurgitated for further mastication, after which it passes into the second two to complete the digestive cycle. The advantage is that the goat may consume food, initially, at a faster rate than if it were to spend long periods masticating, enabling it to move to more protective covering, if required, to consume its food at greater leisure. In the wild essential; for William of 609 even more so.

So where did I spend my early days with these boys? Biggin Hill was an airfield in the county of Kent, the Garden of England, which I thought might really suit me! We were in Kent because someone called Hitler had dictated that his country, called Germany, wanted to occupy my country, called England. We were defending my country — I say *we* because I was important to the boys.

The boys who flew the Spitfires would sit around an area they called a dispersal. It was here they sat, read and waited to be told by someone to 'scramble'. Once they were scrambling they would disappear in their machines. This gave me a bit of freedom to eat and rest, although they did tie me up as they didn't want to lose me.

Out of Jail

When they came back they acknowledged me, but they looked tired and stood or sat around saying things like, 'Hun, bandit, sun and three o'clock,' whilst all the time their hands moved in slow circular motions. Sometimes, one of the boys would not come back; this led to the others looking very sad. I did not understand this – yet. I kind of had company when the boys were away; there was another four-legged creature – a dog called Spit. He was not tied up like me... maybe they did not mind losing him.

Before William arrived to enhance their lives, 609 (West Riding) Squadron had been in existence for five years. Born of Air Ministry Order Number 6/1936, the squadron formed on the 10 February 1936 at RAF Yeadon, near Leeds. Today many people fly and land from the same airfield, but on different missions. It is now the busy commercial, Leeds/Bradford Airport.

In 1924 Lord Trenchard, the founder of the Royal Air Force, had the perception and foresight to recognise that his country faced a threat in Europe and that there was a wealth of untapped potential in the Shires. People who did not want to serve their country full-time, but would on a voluntary part-time basis. He said at a lecture at Cambridge University at the time:

> 'We want the mathematical genius – there is work for him. We want the literary genius – there is work for him. We want the scientific brain – there is work for him. We want the man of brain, we want the man of common sense and little brain, we want the man of action, the methodical man – even the crank...'[1]

But no mention of Goats.

No doubt all of those types of people filled the ranks of 609. Except for the 'regular' training staff, the volunteers came from the West Riding of Yorkshire and most from within ten miles of the city centre of Leeds. The officers generally came from that stratum of society associated with the gentry; the Earl of Lincoln was an early

---

[1] Lecture given by Lord Trenchard, speaking at Cambridge to the Aeronautical Society in 1924.

Out of Jail

Adjutant. The other ranks came from the Leeds area; they were known as Erks. Regardless, as the German political and military machines flexed its muscles, the squadron trained hard in anticipation of the expected conflict. Early aircraft were the Hawker Hart and Hawker Hind, both trainer and bomber variants. In 1939 they received the Supermarine Spitfire and their operational history began.

From Yeadon to Catterick, then Catterick to Drem on the Scottish Coast, they moved as a complete squadron – the reservists were at war. In those early days of the war, 609 patrolled the north east coast of England and the east of Scotland.

Life moved quickly in those days and 609 moved south in 1940 to cover the retreat from Dunkirk before distinguishing itself in the Battle of Britain from bases at Warmwell, Middle Wallop and Hornchurch. It became a battle-hardened squadron, but many of the volunteer aircrew had gone and it was now regulars from all parts of the world who were flying the coveted Spitfire. The first Spitfire Squadron to claim one hundred enemy aircraft was credited to 609. However, most of the Erks were still from Yorkshire – for now. So it was that in 1941 the squadron was at Biggin Hill; the Battle of Britain had been won and Hitler was turning his attention elsewhere.

I did not know where I came from, but liked to think that there was some Yorkshire blood in me somewhere. I have told you that I was a British Toggenburg variety of goat, Latin: *Capra Hircus*, and that my ancestors probably came from Greece or Asia Minor. However, this really does not matter to me or to my boys, but I thought you might like to know.

Life at Biggin Hill was busy – not for me you realise, but for the boys. I was young and spent my formative days learning the ways of man. I lived in and around the dispersal. This place had some comfortable things for me to sit on and a large blackboard on the wall, which had writing on it; the boys looked at this a lot. They also sat around a lot too and waited to be told to go to their aircraft.

Out of Jail

It was a friendly place with plenty for me to explore, because that is what I liked to do. Oh yes, and eat. Grass, plants and flowers surrounded the dispersal and naturally I like all of those. Inside was some lovely smelling stuff on the tables, which was white and thin and often stacked in edible piles. I tried it early on – liked it, but when I went for more I was shouted at. Paper, I discovered by default, was important to some of the boys. Vicki looked after me and made sure I received the liquids that are so essential to an important goat's life. The weaning continued and the slightly bitter, brown liquid I now received by bottle was a delight. It made me feel good; better than the white stuff they initially gave me.

So, I was settling in to the new life and the boys were beginning to realise how special I was. So special in fact that when they talked about moving they said that I was to go with them. Now, climbing is natural to me and so the move into the back of this lorry type of thing was no problem, although the boys thought it might be. The journey was not far and when I arrived at our destination, I found out that I was to live with my boys in a big house.

Gravesend

In August 1941 the squadron moved approximately twenty miles 'up the road' to Gravesend, which was a satellite station for Biggin Hill. The officers were to be billeted in Cobham Hall, which itself had an illustrious history. At that time it was the seat of the Earl of Darnley, a stately house built in Tudor times. Commandeering these fine places was commonplace at this time and provided a comfortable environment for the aircrew between missions. Cobham Hall had been a favourite of Queen Elizabeth I, who used it frequently as an overnight resting place, and of Charles Dickens, who regularly walked through its grounds to the Leather Bottle Pub in Cobham Village. Most importantly, however, for our story – it boasted a wide variety of plants and grasses, including a myriad of rare, tasty bulbs. Today it is an independent boarding school for Girls.

I liked my new home and I was made most welcome. Even the most important person at Gravesend came to meet me. He had two thick stripes more than me and everyone called him 'Marshall'. When the boys went to their machines, I tried to follow but was usually tethered outside the new dispersal because they did not want me too close to the aircraft – did they think I might follow them? Although they did sometimes forget to tie me up and, ignoring the aircraft, I made for the dispersal, which was made for me to explore. It had steps and open windows and ledges. Now us goats innately like heights and narrow ledges. Nature took over and I decided to practice walking backwards, thinking I may need to do it for survival one day. It was all so easy, yet below all of the boys and others were watching me, mouths open. I posed, standing very still.

The audience left, so I gave up my game and went back into the building where I knew there would be special food available. Now, I know I said that grass, plants, hay and flowers were my expected diet, but living with these humans threw up many opportunities to supplement my diet. I have already mentioned paper but every day, at a certain time, the room at the bottom of the building had sandwiches in it. They were delicious, but the boys tried to dissuade me from consuming them – something about not being good for me. Did they really think I would not eat them just because they were bad for me? It was also at this time that I had my first taste of those thin white sticks that the boys placed in their mouths and set fire to. This looked a little frightening to me but without the fire they were delicious. They were of course cigarettes and were to become one of my favourite things to eat.

This place called Gravesend was comfortable, probably too comfortable for a goat, but I did not think so. I was regularly shouted at... but I liked the big chair, the sandwiches and of course it did not really matter because they needed me.

After a short and luxurious time at Cobham Hall, I was ushered back into the lorry and was transported back to Biggin Hill. We were not destined to be there for long, but I felt the emotion of sadness for the first time as a goat – even a special one. The boy who weaned me did not come home to feed me one day. It was one of those times at the dispersal when they were all quiet. Vicki Ortmans, who had brought me from the Old Jail, was missing. We are loyal things us goats and that very kind and courageous man was to feed me no more – I had lost my first friend from the boys.

Vicki Ortmans was one of the first of many Belgians to fly with 609. In a short time he became a popular and outstanding character on the squadron, both on the ground and in the air. He was an exceptional aviator, earning the Distinguished Flying Cross (DFC) in quick time. However, in the three months at Biggin Hill, after returning from Gravesend, he was shot down three times and as a result of the first two he ditched into the English Channel, fortunately being rescued by the RAF Air Sea Rescue. However,

Gravesend

his luck was to run out as the third time he was shot down he was not found and was assumed missing in action – presumed dead. However, he did survive this third hit and was picked up by the German Air Sea Rescue becoming a prisoner of war. He did not see William again.

One day everyone on the squadron met on the large concrete square, which formed part of Biggin Hill. They all looked very smart in a different type of uniform. They all walked together past a kind of stage where a person, who must have been important, was stood. He was nearly as important as me because I stood next to the stage with someone holding on to me. I did not pay too much attention to what was happening but I kept a careful eye on my boys. Afterwards they painted another circle on each of my horns. I was now Flight Lieutenant William de Goat – so it was all for me!

In fact, the parade on 14 November 1941 was for the presentation of the Official Squadron Badge by Air Commodore Harold Peake, Director of Public Relations at the Air Ministry. This was particularly poignant as Peake had been the first commanding officer of 609 in 1936. The badge had the white rose of Yorkshire and the crossed hunting horns on it, supported by the words, Tally Ho!

WILD IN LINCOLNSHIRE

On the 19 November 1941, 609 (WR) Squadron moved north to Lincolnshire. It had spent eighteen months continuous service in front-line sectors. It was reckoned at the time that no other front-line squadron had been so active. RAF Digby was the destination. At this time Digby was a Canadian Sector Airfield commanded by a Canadian Group Captain. In comparison to the south this was a quiet unit, principally a training base.

With my special day over, the people of the squadron were busy putting things in boxes and taking things off the wall and putting them in the backs of lorries. Maybe we were off to that comfortable place again. Without Vicki, I was worried they might leave me here on my own but being the Mascot, and special, I should not have worried, although I missed my weaner and mentor.

One day I was untethered and led to an aircraft which was much larger than a Spitfire. It had two engines and a door to which I was led. I jumped in willingly; inside it was dark and narrow and I was tied up again. The aircraft they trusted me with was called a Harrow and I heard my flying companions saying that it carried twenty men plus the crew, but no mention of goats again. I heard the noise of engines, something I had become used to and then we moved – I, however, did not. This was strange, even for a goat. Then we were up in the air; I tried to move around but was restrained. I really *was* special – they even took me flying!

Due to its age, the Handley Page Harrow had been converted into a transport aircraft. The Harrow that transported William belonged to Number 271 Squadron. It had an average speed of about 150 mph and would have taken approximately two hours to take William to RAF Digby to join his 'boys'. RAF Digby stands in the middle of the flat lands of Lincolnshire, nearly fifteen miles from the capital, Lincoln, and ten miles from the nearest town, Sleaford.

From the aircraft, and here I must confess that I kind of enjoyed the flight, I was taken to the guardroom. Apparently, this is where the guards were and it seemed that they wanted help as well. There was plenty of paper for me to eat and they often let me out to eat more natural things. Very close to the guardroom were some very colourful and sweet-smelling flowers. They looked like those that I might have met if I had lived in the mountains, where I would have been if it were not for this war type of thing. How could I resist them? They were just the kind of thing a goat needs *and* they were available. As they entered my stomach, someone, not from my squadron, started shouting at me. They shouted and shouted, so I headed back to the guardroom, where I was locked up.

After a couple of days I was allowed out again, my boys insisting that it was cruel to keep me locked up. Leaving those beautiful flowers alone, because I was a very bright mascot, I tried to find out where my boys were. I could hear their machines, and I missed them.

During my searches I came upon a building and met one of the guards that I knew. He tried to stroke my head but I quickly ran past him and entered this new building, because I really enjoyed exploring new places – there might be food there. When I rushed into the large room, I came upon lots of young ladies who were holding stick-like things in their hands and they were using them to move things around on a large table when told to do so by some lazy men sitting at another table. All over the walls were maps – I knew this because my men had told me what they were in their dispersals. These ladies and their sticks had never seen a goat in their building before and they started making lots of high-pitched noises. They lost control of their sticks and bits of something flew off the table, landing all over the floor. Someone shouted for my friend, the guard, and he came and took me back to the guardroom. I suppose it was at this stage that I decided that all ladies were there to be frightened, but I lived in a man's world so the opportunity to impart fear would be sparse.

After this escapade, the squadron history reported that William was responsible for vectoring Spitfires over Norway and consequently the station commander decided that he was prone to causing too many problems and, furthermore, was eating too many of his favourite flowers. He did not like aircrew, particularly the Auxiliaries and Belgians. Naturally, neither he nor his staff made life easy for them. William was seen as part of the problem, the final straw coming when he raided the WAAF quarters and ate several of their evening clothes. William was banished to Ashby Hall, which is where the Station Commander had billeted the aircrew of 609. It was a reward for William – he was going back to be with his boys!

I was tethered up once we had returned to the guardroom and, after a rest, I was led to a car. This car, I was to find out later was special like me. It was large and just right for me. A short time later I saw some of my boys; they were sitting outside this very splendid, big house. In the grounds were lots of trees and a lake – I thought I might enjoy it here. This was my chance to explore – something us goats were good at and there were lots of stairs for me to climb too.

The boys always left early in the morning to fly their beloved Spitfires and I had to be tethered because Lincolnshire is a big place and they had learnt that I was an explorer and, given the chance, would eat anything. One day, because *they* liked those ladies that I had frightened, they thought *I* might like a friend – they brought me a lady goat. I did not ask them for one and really did not need her; I preferred my family of boys and men. This nanny, for that is what a lady goat is called, with no name came from an army regiment. So she was a mascot as well. The Welch Fusiliers were her owners, because unlike me she did not own her men. She was very white and very well behaved, I think the Army were more disciplined than my boys and they wanted their mascot to be the same. She was boring, and when it became obvious to my boys that I had no interest in her, she was removed.

This nanny was indeed from another world and was in all likelihood a billy! The Welch Fusiliers traditionally have goats as battalion mascots, but they have to be billys. No wonder William was confused! During the period that 609 were at Digby, the 70th (Young Soldier) Battalion of the Fusiliers were billeted in Lincolnshire undertaking guard duties, principally of RAF bases. The 70th was made up of many ex-Borstal boys who were not yet ready for full-time operations. Regiment history tells us that they were in Lincolnshire from January 1941 until June 1942. Within this Battalion there were seven companies and D Company (D Coy) were guarding Digby during 609's time there. Not to be outdone, they acquired their own 'unofficial' goat, while at the same time being tasked with accommodating the 1st Battalion's goat, as they were serving overseas. The 70th found time for two goats. The 1st Battalions goat escaped from its shed in Skegness during January 1942 and was still missing in March – there is no record of the unofficial creature. However, 609's history states that their adjutant kidnapped a goat from the fusiliers to keep William company! The 70th were billeted nearby at Fulbeck and Skegness is over fifty miles away, therefore one can be led to assume, sixty-five years later, that William's unwanted companion was the unofficial mascot of the 70th.

My goat instinct told me that the boys did not really want to be here, there was very little action, whatever they meant by that. They had many parties and I was allowed to take part – the food was excellent and from somewhere they found some very tasty ale.

Their government in exile presented the car to the Belgians on the squadron. It was called the Belgian Barouche and for reasons never explained it was able to refuel at any military unit without question! The Barouche took William to another exquisite house,

Wild in Lincolnshire

Blankney Hall, which was the centre of many of the parties. Marigold, Countess of Londesborough, was the genial host and the squadron officers were indulged on many occasions. She was also Master of the Blankney Hounds and many of the 'boys' sampled the hunt for the first time. William was not allowed to attend.

The people who looked after the mess did not talk to me the same as my boys. They shouted a lot when I was found upstairs and one day one of them kicked me on the back – it hurt. No one was going to do that to me and I decided to find my boys, my friends. I heard the familiar noise of their Spitfires and followed it. Over fields, stopping for some fresh grass, and through some fences I travelled slowly, listening and looking. I eventually saw a friend at the gate of the base – a guard! He burst out laughing and led me quickly into the room, where I was tethered again. The boys were told, but they had other things on their minds. They were moving again. *Good*, I thought, as I really did not like it here, although, I had discovered ladies…

William walked, trotted or whatever, for close on two miles on the day that he was kicked – he was an independent soul.

The Old Jail Pub near Biggin Hill – where it all began

First photos with my boys. Ortmans sits with me.

Close-up of previous photo

CO of RAF Gravesend, Squadron Leader Marshall welcomes me to his base

Growing in confidence… and horns

My boys hunting with the Blankey Hunt

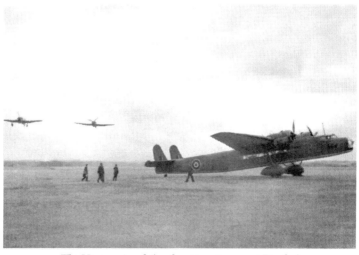
The Harrow aircraft they forgot to put me on at Duxford

Peter Raws – the only shoulders I could stand on!

Me again with Peter and the boys

Peter, I am fed up of your shoulders

Give me some more white sticks! Pierre 'Junior' Soesman (Belgium) obliging.

A Distinguished Flying Cross investiture at RAF Manston – I am unimpressed!

John Steinbeck admires me

*RAF Lympne. Squadron Leader Patrick Thornton-Brown DFC.
The most lovable young man I have ever met.*

*I congratulate 'Pinkie' Stark (with book)
on shooting down the squadron's 200th victim*

*Patrick Thornton-Brown announces my promotion to Group Captain
at a party at the Majestic in Folkestone*

Charles Demoulin (Belgium) proving he has no shoulders

Lympne, just before D-Day

Thorney Island – guarding the Typhoons from a stray dog, just before D-Day

Plumetot in Normandy – resting after being shot at

Boys with commandeered transport in Normandy – not big enough for me

Plantlunne, Germany. My boys and men on 8 May 1945 – Victory in Europe Day. I am so proud of them.

Wuntsdorf, Germany. The last known picture of William – a reluctant hero!

LEFT BEHIND

After only nine months at RAF Digby, the squadron was on the move again, this time to RAF Duxford in Cambridgeshire.

Where was my aircraft? I knew the boys were moving somewhere and I knew I was going with them. The owner of the station and of the guardroom would not let me stay at Digby on my own! Instead of an aircraft, I was shoved into the back of a big truck-like vehicle, a bigger lorry than the one that had taken me on my short journey at Biggin Hill. It was packed with lots of anything – rope, bags, boxes – but nothing for goats. I only had space to sit down; I was grumpy and very uncomfortable.

After travelling along many roads and for what appeared to be a long time, the truck stopped and the driver came to the back and encouraged me to jump out. Jump? I climbed down, but he was not to know. He held my harness and I stretched, attended to nature and found some grass on the side of the road. That was the last stop before I was reunited with my boys. They seemed excited. They were at that place called dispersal but in a different place. Like the other stations I was destined to spend many hours in this particular place. It was where they all congregated – so it was right that I should be there as well. There were no stairs here, so initially I was tethered outside with plenty of grass to eat, supplemented with cigarettes and any paper I could find. The boys, when not excited, stroked me and sat with me. They moved their hands around a lot and I thought they were talking about my flight to that place called Digby, but soon I realised that is what they did when they talked about flying their machines. So, their hands flew as well! It was a quiet place for me, because the boys were away flying for much of the time.

Left Behind

At RAF Duxford, 609 (WR) Squadron, was in the process of replacing the beloved Spitfire with the new and somewhat untested Hawker Typhoon. At one stage they had an equal number of both. The Typhoon was designed as a fighter-bomber, with a potent weapon load. It had many doubters in the Ministry, but Commanding Officer Bee Beamont of 609 believed in its potential and set about proving to them the value of the Typhoon. It became one of the most potent fighter-bombers of the last three years of the war, due in no small part to the dedication and flying skills of 609. They flew it for the rest of the war and William was to become very attached to it. It was a quiet time, operationally, but the pace was gathering.

There was excitement one day and I knew from my vast experience that the boys were preparing to move again. The dispersal building emptied and the men who did not fly came along with lorries and filled them with everything and anything. I was looking forward to my next flight. The day after the lorries had been filled, my boys all left the dispersal together. I heard many noises as their aircraft left the ground and I waited for them to come back, or for the lorry to come to take me to my aircraft. I waited for many hours, goat hours of course. The hours grew into goat days; they had forgotten to take their mascot with them! It was to be a great mistake.

Someone noticed me on my own and, no doubt seeing how sad I looked, took me to that guardroom place, the same type of place that I had been sent to at the last place. My sadness would not disappear though – my boys had gone, and I missed them. Someone with double V-shaped stripes on his sleeve soon befriended me. He took me for walks and fed me with whatever he could find. I helped myself to some paper but longed for some cigarettes. My new friend did not know of my peculiar tastes. I, naturally, became restless and needed a lot more exercise than this kind guard could give me. The guardroom was no place for such a special goat. I now had two thick stripes and one thin one on my growing horns, which I now knew were very important. We goats

Left Behind

have very little perception of time, but I seemed to have stayed in the guardroom for many nights. In my frustration, I occasionally ran about and knocked things all over the place. The man in charge always seemed to be annoyed with me, but he only had one thin stripe on his arm so I was obviously more important than him and so I continued to do as I liked.

The man with the double Vs, Corporal George Clough, began to take me out more and when he took me during the night he would tell me that I had to be quiet and not try to break out. He was kind, but he didn't really understand the nature of a goat. As I grew sadder and with thoughts that I might not see my boys again, one of them suddenly appeared one day, without warning. Not one of the real boys, as this one did not fly, but he worked with the paper that I really liked eating. After talking to my guard, they found a car and the three of us were off!

Away from the base we moved quickly along narrow roads – where was I going? Eventually the boy from my squadron took me out of the car and we moved to a platform type of place. Corporal Clough patted me on the head and stroked me many times, and then I heard this strange noise. A kind of chuntering and hissing, it moved closer and louder until a large vehicle with smoke coming out of it approached the platform. Behind this steaming, chuntering machine were many other types of vehicles. Most had windows in and from those windows, not all of them, people looked out. The whole thing stopped and my boy took me down the platform and opened a door. We entered a kind of room with no windows and no furniture, but it did have a small gap that let in some light. The steam thing made a lot of noise and we began to move, but again I did not. I thought that we might take off and fly. Not so, as for some time we moved with a kind of rolling motion, occasionally stopping. No more goats joined me, but then again I was special. At one stop my boy untied me, opened the door and led me down another platform – I'd been brought to another new place. Another journey in a car followed, but suddenly I heard the familiar noise of aircraft and I was soon back with my boys. They

37

were all very friendly – most were familiar, some were new, but I was home. They painted over the thin stripe with a thick one – I now had three!

The sympathetic policeman, Corporal George Clough, who knew that the adjutant at Duxford wanted to supply a local farmer with this troublesome goat, had looked after William. He would undoubtedly have ended up as food. During the weeks that 609 flew without William, the operational effectiveness waned significantly. Following a short period back at Biggin Hill, the squadron moved to RAF Manston with its Typhoons. As things deteriorated, one of the aircrew mentioned that maybe, just maybe, it was the fact that William was not with them. This sentiment was initially ignored, but their operational and personnel problems did not improve and so the adjutant was asked to contact Duxford to ascertain whether William was still alive. Fortunately, he was. The butcher's knife had not claimed him. William owed his life to the policeman, Corporal George Clough.

After corresponding with Duxford, the adjutant was dispatched north to bring William home. The rail journey from Whittlesey to Ramsgate cost 10/1d for William and it was worth every penny. The squadron's fortunes improved immediately and on William's return, the commanding officer stated that he would never be allowed to leave the squadron again.

The following are two letters sent at the time between Duxford and Manston NAFDU:

RAF Station Duxford
Cambs

20 November 1942

Dear Ziegler (609 Intelligence Officer)

On the 18th I sent you a signal saying that the goat would leave Whittlesford at 1201 (hours). I sent the signal but forgot to send the goat! However, it really has left Whittlesford now, bound for

Left Behind

Ramsgate Station, and I have sent another signal today letting you know that it is on its way.

Enclosed is a railway form which when decoded means that you owe me 10/1d!

Yours aye

Charles Guthrie

*

NAFDU
RAF Station Duxford
Cambs

5 December 1942

Dear Ziegler

Thank you very much for your letter of the 2 December and for enclosing a postal order for 10/-d. I am glad that the goat arrived safely, and I trust that it will bring your squadron great luck.

Yours aye

Charles Guthrie

Typhoon Boys

My new home was a really good place for me to be. The boys were very keen to be with me and they were always feeding me with their type of food and putting me near good and tasty grass, which was my type of food. I was never far away from the dispersal building. As you know, I liked these dispersal-type buildings because out of them came food and, of course, this is where the boys hung out. By this time they spent much more time stroking me and talking to me, and they also gave me some new things to eat. There were more of the cigarettes, unlit of course. Being a goat, albeit a very special one, I took them and ate them – no setting fire to it for me – that seemed a waste. These tasted more bitter than I remembered but I did not really care. They were tastier than grass. I let the boys stroke me even more when they gave me these white sticks. This only encouraged them to give me more. I was becoming a very clever mascot!

I experienced another delightful taste purely by chance. One day I was allowed near one of the aircraft, I think they wanted me to climb onto it – maybe to fly in it. I noticed some liquid falling from a place near the front – it had an interesting smell and being an inquisitive goat, I tried it. The liquid was different to anything I had tasted before and I wanted more.

William had discovered glycol-cooling fluid, which was used in the engines of the Typhoon. Once he had the taste and if allowed, he would stand for hours feeding off the drips. However, 'more bitter' cigarettes were still his favourites. Reliable information claimed they were the brand, Players. He was becoming fussy.

They were busy now – my boys. They sat in a machine called a Typhoon and like the Spitfire went into the air in it. I was not lonely though; I had a new friend who did not fly. He looked after me when the boys were not there. Like my friend at the last place, he had a double V on his arm. Some days, if the weather was not good, the boys stayed with me and played games around me. Once, a tall man with very big shoulders taught me to climb onto them. Now, I was a natural climber and so this was normal for me, but they seemed to enjoy themselves when I did this. They would shout and laugh, and this became one of their favourite games — although some could not mange it. One of the boys who was very good at it was Peter Raw. He was like a mountain and I enjoyed climbing onto his shoulders. He was my new friend; he looked after me and understood my climbing abilities.

Peter Raw was an ex-army officer, who had transferred into the RAF to fly. A larger than life character, he had played good class rugby, giving him the shoulders to befriend William. He was an extremely able aviator, but like many of his peers he lost his life in action on the 21 March 1944.

Some were not so mountainous, but they were easily pleased, I thought. Another day, when they were not in the air, one of the boys came up to me carrying a large, hard, tube-type of thing. On one end was a kind of nipple — now that is natural — so I put my mouth over it. What happened next was most unusual. I felt something enter my mouth and throat — just a taste — nothing solid. It felt good, but I began to feel larger and full of wind, so when they took the nipple away, I began to do what all animals do, naturally, when full — I released air from my rear end! Running around made this process easier and my boys encouraged me to do this. They just stood around — all in good form. So they enjoyed it as well. Life was very good for me in this very busy place.

William and 609 were now at RAF Manston, close to Ramsgate on the Isle of Thanet. Situated on the extremity of eastern Kent; Manston was significantly close to mainland Europe. William was promoted to wing commander, which made him the highest-ranking officer on the squadron. With William safely returned to them, his squadron enjoyed great success, and under the leadership of Bee Beamont, 609 took part in raids over occupied France, destroying the communications infrastructure and inventing, then perfecting, the technique of 'train busting'.

Emery Pearce, writing for the *Daily Herald* in March 1943, wrote about William being awarded the Distinguished Service Order (DSO) for his significant presence, and in allowing the squadron to become successful again. Pearce also noted that William was awarded the Distinguished Flying Cross (DFC), because on the first day after the commanding officer had made it an order to salute William, the squadron shot down six aircraft! William's DFC was well received and saluting him became a ritual, because if they did not they would have no luck that day! His guardian was Corporal Summerscales, one of the last auxiliaries on the squadron and now one of the most important people. The squadron was conducting sorties on a daily basis over the coast of Northern France, Belgium and Holland. Little did they know at the time, but they were part of the preparations to invade and release Europe from occupation. The men of the West Riding Squadron were making a name for themselves and it was not unusual for them to be singled out for visits by VIPs and the press. William was invited to all the visits and special occasions – he was now inseparable from his boys.

Most days for me were a round of eating, resting, being patted by the boys and being taken for walks by the man with double V on his shoulder. I had my own hut behind the dispersal and it even had my name on it – so I knew where to go. If I was not up too early and the boys were around, some would come and see me and stroke me before raising their arm to salute me as I was now more senior than them, before going off to fly. Some days were different however, and this was usually when someone I did not know came to the dispersal to meet the boys. Most stood with them and moved their hands and arms around – copying my boys. Some did not and just stood and talked. Some stood and pointed at me, which of course they should have done – I was special after all. One in particular spent a lot of time next to me. He kept touching my head, my fur and my horns. I did not mind because I was helping him out in some way – and he might feed me some nice tit-bits. He spoke differently to most of the boys; he had a twangy accent, which I didn't consider normal.

The 'twangy' accent belonged to John Steinbeck, an American war reporter working with the *Daily Express*. His brief was to report on this famous fighter squadron and its exploits. To everyone's surprise the paper published an article on 15 August 1943 about the goat that everyone saluted. After the war the author, who gained fame with many books including *The Grapes of Wrath*, wrote a book of short stories titled *Men at War*. This book contained a chapter on the only non-human to be recorded – William.

Here follows extracts from the *Daily Express* Article:

> His name is Wing Commander William Goat, DSO, DFC, and he is old in honours and some say in iniquity, but when he joined the RAF two years ago he was just able to totter about on his long and wobbly legs … He will eat nearly everything. No party or any review is complete without him. At one party it is reported that being left alone for a few moments, he ate 200 sandwiches, three cakes and the arrangements of 'Pomp And Circumstance' … He has the confidence of his men … This goat has only one truly bad habit – he loves beer, and furthermore, he is able to absorb it in such quantities … In appearance this goat is not impressive. He has shabby, pinkish fur and a cold and fish-like eye. His legs are not straight, in fact he is slightly knock-kneed.[1]

Just like they did at Biggin Hill, the boys and men occasionally stood together on the large piece of concrete near the dispersal. They were in blocks of three rows and after standing still for a while they would come past me all together doing a funny walk. I stood with my double V friend and took their salute. So did

---

[1] John Steinbeck, 'Commander Goat, D.S.O.', *Daily Express*, 15 July, 1943.

someone else, who had come to visit us. He stood close to me on a platform; I think it was to let him see over me. After some walking, the squadron stood still and together again. One of the boys would then walk towards me, stop and salute. The man behind me stepped forward and pinned a round piece of metal onto the chest of the boy. As he walked past me the other important person tickled my chin. Then it was off for food and drink. It was all a bit of a tedious thing really, but my boys wanted me there and the food was most welcome afterwards so I didn't really mind.

The important person for this parade at Manston was the commanding officer of Number 11 Group, Air Vice Marshal 'Dingbat' Saunders and he was there to present the Distinguished Flying Cross to Flying Officer 'Cheval' Lallemand. Cheval became one of three Belgians to Command 609 during the war. Visitors continued to seek out 609 and their now famous mascot.

Relief in the Air

The squadron moved to Lympne in August of 1943 and it was from here that they accounted for their 200th enemy aircraft. It was during a sortie over France and 'Pinkie' Stark, later to become the last wartime commanding officer of 609, was the pilot that accounted for a Junkers JU 88.

My new home was very luxurious, it was owned by a man called Sir Philip Sassoon and was surrounded by lots of grass and trees and plants and everything else that I liked. It also had a large piece of water, which the boys spent a lot of their time sitting around when they were not in the Typhoon. The new senior boy was a very friendly man and I spent a lot of time with him – he obviously needed me more than the others. His name was Pat Thornton-Brown. The boys were extremely busy now and I did not see as much of them as I had before. But they never forgot me and always made sure that I had enough of the luxury foods and drinks to keep me happy. My guardian was very kind to me and he regularly took me to the place where he worked – but I was not allowed inside, apparently there was too much temptation for me – he remembered that I liked paper.

One day there was great excitement and the boys were full of something. One of them received lots of pats – or was it slaps – and posed for many pictures. Of course they wanted me in them – they always did. Soon after this day, we all went to a big house in a town called Folkestone. It had a massive hall and was full of people. Most were from the squadron, but there were also many of those of the female variety. After my usual drinks and white sticks I circulated rapidly around this huge hall, knocking a few of those females off their feet – just like my boys. Of course when the most important boy said a few words I was supposed to be at his side – even though I felt a little unsteady at this stage, which was not

Relief in the Air

good with four knobbly legs. He had to speak without me — I cannot remember where I was.

This most special occasion was the celebration party to commemorate the 200th enemy aircraft shot down by 609. The Air Officer Commanding Number 11 Group sent a signal 'releasing 609 from duty until such time as the CO decides it is capable of taking over again.'[1]

Staged at the Majestic Hotel in Folkestone over 600 people and one goat attended. William was now a celebrity and by the end of the night he was a Group Captain. It was a night of celebration and mayhem and the squadron records of the day say, 'Amongst the sea of humanity, consuming cigarettes and nodding patronisingly to airmen, stalks at intervals the dignified and sacred figure of W/C de Goat, DSO, DFC.'[2]

When at last the CO was reluctantly persuaded to make a short speech, the Wing Commander could not be found. The CO, after pointing out that the 100th Hun met disaster on its way to London and the 200th on its way to Paris, announced the promotion of W/C de Goat to acting Group Captain — news which made headlines in the *Daily Express* the next day.

I did not move much the next day and neither did the boys. This was not to last for too long however, as they became busy again. We were soon on the move. No sooner had I discovered my favourite grass and dispersal than my friend was putting me inside one of those large lorries that they now used for everything. Where was my plane? I am a Group Captain now! My wish soon came true, but it was all so rushed, they pushed me onto my favourite aircraft so quickly that I did not have time to relieve myself. So, halfway through the journey, I let it be known in no uncertain goat terms that I had a requirement to relieve myself. Rapidly opening

---

[1] Quote taken from the Squadron F540. This is a record written at the time by, in this case, the Squadron Intelligence Officer. Once a Squadron or Unit disbands, the Air Historical Branch keeps the F540. 609 have a copy of the wartime F540.
[2] As above.

one of the doors one of the men placed me as close as he could to the door and despite the rush of wind from outside, I managed to let go. They never rushed me onto a plane again!

The squadron had been deployed to Llanbedr in North Wales to perfect its rocket firing technique. At the last moment the ground crew and medical officer were tasked with bringing William to the ranges. He was boarded onto an old Sparrow aircraft, (a derivative of William's beloved Harrow) which had lost a door and consequently William was tethered to a strut in the fuselage. While cruising over some town, William decided to empty his bowel and a trail of little black bullets disappeared out of the doorway. The orderly was heard to say, 'That will be black rain for some poor sod.'

On 1 April 1944, 609 arrived at Thorney Island. It was to be the last base they served on in the United Kingdom during the Second World War.

Here, at yet another new home for me, I felt a bit lonely. There was my friend, but the boys were so busy that I did not see very much of them. When I did join them they made sure I was looked after and fed me plenty of white sticks and if they had more time they would bring one of those hard tubes which gave me the chance to suck on something very nice and then run around wildly, while releasing plenty of wind. They enjoyed making me play with them at times and would tease me by offering things I liked and then taking them away just as I went to eat them. The more they did this the more I pretended to be angry and I would scrape the ground with my front legs and lower my horns in a show of wanting to charge someone. It was always good fun and on one occasion they even pushed me into a room of visitors and I chased them all out with my horns. The boys laughed loudly.

Quentin Reynolds, an illustrious US Army journalist, led the visitors. The aircrew had had enough of visitors and decided to use William to disturb them. It worked; William was not a discerning type of goat – he did the dirty work for his keepers.

Relief in the Air

It was soon after this bit of fun that I began to feel sick. It was the first time I had felt like this during my goat time with the boys. It started with me not wanting to eat – even the delicious stuff that the boys had put on my imposing horns. These were my promotion stripes and I now had four thick ones. It was easy food – a stroke of my front leg across the horns followed by a tasty licking of my knobbly leg. They tried everything I had become partial to, but the boys grew concerned when I refused the white sticks. They must have begun to panic because I was so important to them. Consequently, I heard them asking someone who knew about these things to look at me. This man touched me, held a small metal thing on various parts of my body, which was cold, and then he sat down in front of me and read a book. After a while the delicacy on my horns disappeared and was not replaced. I thought they were being unkind and demoting me, but I stopped feeling sick and was soon eating everything again.

The 'new' Medical Officer (MO) Doc Bell was informed at his arrival interview on posting, that he was also responsible for the welfare of William. This came as a surprise to the doctor, who quite naturally had no experience of this kind of creature. William was different and the squadron needed him to be well. The MO was a quick learner and established that the paint being used to indicate his rank – Blue Dope – was slowly poisoning him. It was taken off immediately. Doc Bell writes in his book, *To Live Among Heroes*[3] the following:

> The goat had been quite ill when I saw him for the first time but the removal of the paint assured his return to good health and a normal diet of grass, paper, cigars, cigarettes and portions of unconsumed breakfast, lunch, dinner which his personal assistant and others brought to him. No one on the squadron thought it odd that when someone was offering a round of cigarettes, Billy was included or if some important document went missing in the orderly room, the excuse that, 'Billy must have eaten it' were accepted without question.

The MO added another patient to his list.

---

[3] Bell, George Armour, To Live Amoung Heroes, Grub Street, 2001, p17.

INTO EUROPE

The squadron was now extremely busy on operations, preparing the way for the anticipated invasion of mainland Europe.

It was a very different time for me. The boys seemed to be busier than they ever had been. Although, they did not ignore me and continued to raise their arm when they passed me. They did not entertain or touch me as much as they once did, but I sort of realised that something different was happening. Even the men who looked after the machines that the boys sat and flew in were very busy. My guardian did not come to me as often as he used to; until one day, I think it was early in the morning, he rushed up to me, untethered me and led me across the fields to a much larger aircraft than I had ever seen before. This time he made sure I relieved myself – there were no open doors on this aircraft. Buzzing around it were many of the men, placing and throwing bits of anything into the doors. It seemed chaotic – even to a goat. At last, after I had chewed on some very tasty grass, I was encouraged to leap into this very large aircraft. It was packed full of everything and already had a few people in. They had left a space for me, but it was a small one. The doctor who had helped me when I felt sick was with us – so I felt sure that they were going to look after me.

No sooner had I bedded down than the bump of landing happened – I knew this because I was an experienced flying goat. I stood up slowly and then suddenly everyone on the aircraft started shouting. Someone grabbed me and as the door opened they jumped, hoping I would follow – I did. He ran and again I followed. I could hear large and small explosions. He was shouting and then he suddenly jumped into a kind of long hole. I naturally followed, landing on top of this someone. Inside this hole were lots of other people — all shouting and holding their hands on top of their hats, which were on their heads. I decided to explore as we goats are entitled to. Those men that did not know me seemed to want to shout at me even more. After a short time, or so it seemed, the noises ceased.

One of the airmen of 609, Airman Barker-Keukens, recalled in a letter over fifty years later that he was on the DC3 Dakota, an American transport aircraft in service with the RAF that took William and squadron equipment to Normandy. They landed at Plumetot (B10) on the 1 July 1944. He said:

> We landed at one of the makeshift landing strips in a cloud of dust and sand and dry earth. As soon as the aircraft stopped we leapt out and made a beeline for the nearest slit trench, which were scattered around the strip. The reason for our rushing was that Jerry was shelling/mortaring the strip from close by. I dragged William with me and pulled him down on top of me in the trench, much to the consternation of the 'bods' who, were already in occupation. This all happened in the space of perhaps five minutes and when the shelling stopped we emerged from the trench and ran into a nearby copse. Not so William, he decided to go in the opposite direction. That was it — we were in France.

It was nearly a week before the aircraft of 609 arrived, but William had a lot to explore.

Now, it is thought that us goats only think on a day-to-day basis. In fact, that may be what everybody thinks about all of us four-legged creatures. I only know about me and I am a most different goat, indeed I am Group Captain William de Goat. A very senior officer and fully entitled to my rations of the white sticks and those hard tubes with some blowing up stuff in them.

It will not surprise you to hear that I was now in a different world. Everything was happening and everybody rushed about, always doing things. I saw little of my boys in this different world and even my guardian was only seen occasionally. There were no buildings to explore and the days of playing games had gone. The boys that were with me lived in canvas type of things, which did not seem too comfortable. One day, a group of people, mainly of the lady variety, arrived dressed all in black. They waved their arms around in front of me and some of my boys – I just looked at them. They were ladies but I was not in the mood to chase them, they looked sad. The men tried to talk to them, but they spoke a different type of language. One of our Belgian boys eventually spoke to them; he was clever because he spoke the same kind of language. The ladies left slowly, shuffling their feet with heads bowed.

Allan Billam, a Typhoon pilot with the squadron, who also travelled to Normandy at the same time as William, remembers that the locals were fascinated as 609 arrived complete with a goat, and not just any old goat of course.

> The peasant ladies sent a deputation, requesting Billy's services to sire their next batch of goats. We left it to the Belgians in the squadron to explain tactfully that Billy did not have the necessary equipment, having been neutered at an early age.

This surely explains William's four-year disdain for the young ladies of the war world!

I had just become familiar with the nooks and crannies of this place, which had led me to the tastiest grass and plants, when one of the men from the squadron arrived, untied me, took me to a lorry and encouraged me into the back of it. Once aboard we moved. We did not go far, but as we moved there were the noises of explosions all around us. The roads were full and movement was slow. We moved through villages that looked in a very poor state. The people from these places just stood and stared at me. They were not dressed the same as my men. I know I was special, but why did they stare? This type of day continued; some days we moved a long way and some days not. We always arrived at a new place; some had buildings and some did not. At all of them I had to find

Into Europe

plants and grass and just hope that my boys and men would remember to give me my white sticks. Sometimes they did and sometimes they did not. They were very busy, my boys. Even the tasty paper seemed to have been taken away. Moving and packing and moving again seemed to be what my friends were doing.

From landing in Normandy on 1 July 1944, until the cessation of hostilities in May 1945, 609 unpacked and packed at twelve different bases. Movement of the complete squadron occurred nearly every month, often under attack. This in itself was a major logistics problem. The Allied Forces moved through Northern Europe and 609, as part of the Second Tactical Air Force, supported Montgomery's ground forces as they advanced through France, Belgium, Holland (where William was promoted to air commodore at Gilze Rijen) and finally into Germany. William was never left behind; he was part of the inventory. By the nature of the operations, it was inevitable that he would not be in the forefront of activities as he had been in the United Kingdom. All records and books on 609 during this time hardly mention William, but at Merville in Northern France...

My vehicle bumped around and the incessant noise of the rain on the canvas kept me awake. Then, like so many times since my last flight, I was shouted down, had they forgotten that I was a Group Captain? I jumped into a quagmire. My strong legs found it difficult to move, but I was soon with my boys, which was good. I had not seen a lot of them for some time – they did not travel with me in my lorry. Here they gave me my white sticks – oh how I had missed them.

While my boys were away, all remembering to raise their arms to me each morning, I was tied up and one thoughtful boy brought me something to rest upon. It was loose and comfortable, but as I settled down, the smell of good food took over. It was far tastier than restful. Now, some of my favourites had not been available for some time, so I began to consume this wonderfully smelling extra. When it was dark I ate even more, us goats sometimes do not know when to stop. As the light slowly came across the mud, I began to feel like I was a much bigger goat, which was not unusual for me. Unlike the other times with the hard tubes, I was not able to release the wind or run around. I felt miserable and in pain. I called for help in my own bleating way. The boys laughed at me, but summoned the man who was there to look after me, and he did. The tasty stuff was moved away.

William had been tethered near a large heap of ersatz stuffing that had once filled some old mattresses from a nearby barrack block. It looked like wood shavings and was meant for him to sleep on – not eat!

It was here, in the mud, that I first felt that most dangerous of emotions, jealousy. For a couple of days or so, my boys ignored me except for their raising of hands early in the morning. When not in their machines and not eating or drinking, they seemed to stand around a type of small wooden building, which was near to their eating and sleeping place. I decided to take a look one day when the boys were in their machines. As I approached I heard lots of high-pitched squealing. I could see nothing, but us goats can climb with ease; I put my front legs on top of the building and looked in with my most staring look. There was a small creature, pinkish underneath the dirt and with a short, stubby nose. He was very small and a mess, but he took my boys away from me. As much as I tried, my attempts to teach the small creature a lesson proved to be too difficult, then one day he was gone. My boys obviously knew I was the most important creature and they were soon concentrating on me again. Soon after, I was being told to climb into my lorry – we were leaving the mud behind.

William had met, and been jealous of, Herman. He was a small pig that had been acquired by some New Zealand pilots after a night out in nearby Calais. They were not of 609 and not being such caring folk, brought Herman back to the Officers' Mess with a view to Christmas in mind rather than in sympathy for a war orphan. One of the 'rescuers' was Desmond Scott a highly decorated New Zealand pilot, who, at Merville and at the age of twenty-five, was a Group Captain commanding 123 Wing, of which 609 was a part.

He said of the time:

> However there was one member of the Wing that could not stand the sight of 'Herman' and that was Billy the goat. He had obviously made up his mind that France was not big enough for both of them and we had to cover the pigsty with strong reinforced wire netting. Billy would spend hours trying to find a way into 'Herman's' little house and we often saw him standing at full stretch on his hind legs looking down into the pig's straw-floor bunker. You could read the message in his eyes.'[1]

Unlike William, Herman was destined to be sacrificed to supplement the Christmas fayre. Little was heard of William after this, but he was always with the squadron. Movement was rapid throughout Holland and the squadron arrived in Germany in May.

Plantlunne, just across the border from Holland, was the place to be on 8 May 1945. This was Victory in Europe Day and 609 were all together and not required to fly on operations or to move. William was very much part of the day.

After a lot of travelling and lonely times, suddenly everything and everybody seemed to stop. We were at a big place and all the boys and all the men were together again. I received my white sticks again, there was brown liquid to be had and I was allowed to seek out my other favourite drink, which fell from the aircraft. We also played again. They did not rush off to their machines and the men did not stand around them. Instead they did things, which I had not seen before. They built big mounds of anything that they collected from the base, stood around them and then, to lots of cheering, set fire to them. There were many mounds. As the mounds burnt some of the men fired things into the air; there were

---

[1] Desmond Scott, *Typhoon Pilot*, Leo Cooper Ltd, 1982.

many different colours and even in goat terms they were pretty but a little bit scary. There was a lot of that beer stuff around and of course they made sure that I was looked after. This kind of thing continued as it became darker and darker. The next time light came I was the only creature on my feet. The rushing around had stopped. I did not see the boys for a long time that day.

The squadron remained in Germany at Wuntsdorf until the Japanese surrendered. Finally, in September 1945 the remnants of 609 (West Riding) Squadron returned to the United Kingdom to follow most wartime units into disbandment. Lasham in Hampshire was the disbandment base. William flew back with them and after landing, the remaining aircrew sat with him and patted him and stroked him. A last round of cigarettes was offered before William was presented to a local farmer. The farmer was well briefed about how special he had become and that he should be treated as a war hero.

My last view of my boys was of them raising their arms as this new man in my life led me away to a large field. He seemed a person who would care for me. The grass was tasty and he stroked me a lot. I knew that my life was going to change. No more cigarettes, no more glycol, no more being blown up by a tube and no more paper. Above all however, no more of my boys company. They had been very special friends and without doubt I had enhanced their very full lives.

One hopes that William had a peaceful and contented retirement on the farm. One suspects that he missed everything that was different and which he had adopted supporting his boys as they put their lives on the line every day, bringing freedom back to Europe. If there is a goat heaven then one hopes that William is there, chewing on a cigarette and keeping a keen eye on all his 609 boys.

Tally Ho!

Printed in Great Britain
by Amazon